The Cute Quiche

Quiches to Fall in Love with France

By: Layla Tacy

License Notes

Table of Contents

Introduction

French food shouldn't intimidate you. It's just food, after all. In fact, the idea of making French food in your kitchen should excite you - especially if it's a quiche! It's extremely easy and the oven does most of the work for you, so why haven't you given this French dish a try? It's not like we're making macarons or choux... It's just a quiche!

Sure, you have to follow certain steps in order to make sure it turns out perfect, but don't you have to follow a recipe for most dishes anyway? With enough practice, you'll be able to eyeball most of the ingredients anyway - but in order to get there, you first need some practice. That's why we're here! "The Cute Quiche" will give you 25 amazing but simple recipes to introduce you to the world of quiches and help you fall in love with the dish. It's easy but complex and delicate on so many levels that whipping one up will have you and all of your guests impressed. The fact that you mostly just let the oven do the cooking for you will be left unspoken because quiche is elegant and fancy enough on its own.

Don't worry if you've never baked one before, though, because our recipes are easy to follow for all level home cooks! Having said that, we could get started right now! We've already taken a look at your fridge and pantry and we've measured out the flour and butter for the crust. All you need to do now is choose a recipe for the filling. So, what's it going to be? We suggest the mushroom and asparagus quiche. Good luck!

xxxxxxxxxxxxxxxxxxxxxxxxxxxxxxxxxxxxxxxxxxxxxxxxxxxxxxxxxx

Mustard Infused Quiche

This incredible quiche uses English mustard in its filling to create an incredible blend of flavors that will leave you asking for more. The mustard and the bacon rashes in the filling create a divine tasting dish that you can enjoy with brunch or afternoon tea.

Serving Size: 6

Duration: 50 minutes.

List of Ingredients:

- 1 cup plain flour
- 4 tbsp. lard
- 1/4 tsp. sea salt
- 1 cup water, refrigerated
- 1 shallot, finely chopped
- 2 bacon rashers, minced
- 1 cup cheese, shredded
- 1/4 tsp. black pepper
- 1 tsp. English mustard
- 2 tbsp. red capsicum, finely chopped
- 1 tomato, chopped
- 4 eggs
- 1 cup whole milk
- 2 tsp. flour

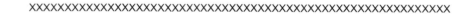

xxxxxxxxxxxxxxxxxxxxxxxxxxxxxxxxxxxxxxxxxxxxxxxxxxxxxxxxx

Directions:

1. Put lard and sea salt in a blender and set to low pulse.

2. Add flour put it on high for 3 minutes.

3. Turn to low pulse and add cold water.

4. Mix until a dough is formed.

5. Roll the uncooked pastry to form a circle.

6. Preheat the kitchen oven to 360°F.

7. Put the shallot and cheese on the pastry base.

8. Add bacon and chopped capsicum.

9. In a deep pot, beat eggs and add mustard.

10. Add flour and milk while stirring and mix until smooth.

11. Place the pastry in a quiche pan and spread egg mixture on top.

12. Add tomatoes and heat in an oven for 45 minutes.

Tex-Mex Quiche

The olive and cheese filling of this quiche makes it perfect for brunch. It does away with protein and includes olives, so even those who adhere to the vegan diet can take a bite and enjoy its glorious taste.

Serving Size: 6

Duration: 40 minutes

List of Ingredients:

- 1 tsp. chili powder
- 1 pie shell, uncooked
- 1 cup Monterey Jack cheese, shredded
- 1 cup cheddar cheese, shredded
- 1 tbsp. flour
- 3 eggs, whisked
- 1 and a half cup half-and-half
- 1 can green chilies, finely chopped
- 1 can olives, pitted and chopped
- 1 tsp. sea salt
- 1/4 tsp. black pepper

xxxxxxxxxxxxxxxxxxxxxxxxxxxxxxxxxxxxxxxxxxxxxxxxxxxxxxxxxxx

Directions:

1. Spread the chili powder on the inside of the pie shell.

2. Put and Monterey Jack cheese and cheddar cheese in a bowl.

3. Add flour and mix well.

4. Place mixture in pie shell.

5. Put in eggs and cream.

6. Stir gently and add chilies and olives.

7. Season with salt and pepper.

8. Add cheese.

9. Heat in an oven at 325°F for 45 minutes.

10. Cool before cutting into wedges.

Crustless Quiche

This is a unique take on the traditional quiche recipe. It does away with the crust and creates an incredible pseudo-crust instead. Your guests will be amazed at your finesse when you serve them this dish.

Serving Size: 4

Duration: 30 minutes

List of Ingredients:

- 2 eggs
- 1 cup whole milk
- 1 cup cheese, shredded
- 1 cup mushrooms, finely chopped
- 1/2 a cup, flour
- 1/2 a cup spring onions, minced
- 1 tsp. sea salt
- 1 tsp. black pepper
- 1 tomato, finely chopped

xxxxxxxxxxxxxxxxxxxxxxxxxxxxxxxxxxxxxxxxxxxxxxxxxxxxxxxx

Directions:

1. Beat the eggs with the whole milk.

2. Put in the cheese.

3. Put in mushrooms, plain flour, and spring onions. Continue to mix.

4. Put the mixture into a well-oiled quiche pan.

5. Spread chopped tomato over the mixture.

6. Heat in an oven at 365°F for 35 minutes.

Mini Quiche

These small quiches are baked in tins. However, their small size should not fool anyone, for they are incredibly tasty and highly nutritious. The bacon and shallot filling is an incredible combination that tastes incredible.

Serving Size: 4

Duration: 40 minutes

List of Ingredients:

- A Couple of sheets of simple puff pastry
- 2 eggs
- 1 and a quarter cup whole milk
- 1 tomato, finely chopped
- 2 slices bacon, finely chopped
- 2 shallots
- 1/4 cup cheese, shredded
- 1 tsp. sea salt
- 1 tsp. black pepper

xxxxxxxxxxxxxxxxxxxxxxxxxxxxxxxxxxxxxxxxxxxxxxxxxxxxxxxx

Directions:

1. Preheat the kitchen oven to 392°F.

2. Oil a couple of muffin tins.

3. Cut pastry into circles using a biscuit cutter.

4. Place finely chopped bacon with tomato and shallots in each.

5. Whisk the eggs and whole milk.

6. Season with sea salt and black pepper.

7. Sprinkle shredded cheese.

8. Fill each tin with the mixture.

9. Heat in an oven for 15 minutes.

10. Cool the pie slightly on wire rack.

Quiche Lorraine

This quiche hails from the French town of Lorraine, hence its name. Although some consider it to be a tricky dish to prepare and bake, we have included a recipe that will guide you through the pitfalls, and the result will be a perfect Quiche Lorraine.

Serving Size: 4

Duration: 40 minutes

List of Ingredients:

- 2 sheets pastry
- 6 slices bacon, finely chopped
- 1 shallot, finely chopped
- 3 eggs, whisked
- 1 and a 1/2 cup whole milk
- 1/4 tsp. sea salt
- 1/4 tsp. black pepper
- 1 cup cheese, finely grated
- 1 tbsp. plain flour

xxxxxxxxxxxxxxxxxxxxxxxxxxxxxxxxxxxxxxxxxxxxxxxxxxxxxxxxxxxx

Directions:

1. Preheat the kitchen oven to 330°F.

2. Heat bacon and shallot in a skillet until golden brown.

3. Stir together whole milk and sea salt with eggs in a wide, deep pot.

4. Add bacon and chopped shallot.

5. Using a separate deep pot, add cheese and mix in flour. Add this to the eggs.

6. Oil a quiche pan and line it with pastry.

7. Put egg mixture in the crust.

8. Heat in an oven for 40 minutes.

9. Place on a wire rack before serving.

Crab Quiche

This quiche uses imitation crab meat as its filling. Combined with Swiss cheese, it is an incredibly delicious pie. Serve it with grilled asparagus to enjoy it in its perfection.

Serving Size: 6

Duration: 50 minutes

List of Ingredients:

- 1 pastry shell, uncooked
- 1 cup Swiss cheese, shredded
- 1/2 a cup sweet pepper, finely chopped
- 1/4 cup shallots, finely chopped
- 1 tbsp. lard
- 3 eggs
- 1 and a 1/2 cup half-and-half
- 1/2 a tsp. sea salt
- 1/4 tsp. black pepper
- 1 cup imitation crabmeat, finely chopped

Directions:

1. Line pastry shell with foil.

2. Heat in an oven at 445°F for 6 minutes.

3. Heat in an oven 5 minutes more without foil.

4. Spread cheese over crust.

5. Turn down the heat to 375°.

6. In a skillet, heat pepper and shallots in lard till translucent.

7. In a wide pot, whisk together the eggs, cream, salt and pepper.

8. Stir in the crab, and remaining cheese.

9. Put into crust.

10. Heat in an oven for 35 minutes.

11. Place on a wire rack before cutting.

Tangy Bacon Quiche

This quiche is one of the most visually stunning quiche dishes that you can make. It can be served as a main course in even the poshest of menus, or you can cook it for brunch and enjoy it with your family.

Serving Size: 4

Duration: 40 minutes

List of Ingredients:

- 4 eggs
- 1 and a 1/2 cup whole milk
- 3 tbsp. lard
- 1/2 a cup flour
- 1 and a 1/2 cup cheese, shredded
- 1 cup bacon rashers, finely minced

xxxxxxxxxxxxxxxxxxxxxxxxxxxxxxxxxxxxxxxxxxxxxxxxxxxxxxxx

Directions:

1. Preheat oven to 356°F.

2. Mix lightly beaten eggs, with whole milk in a deep pot.

3. Add the lard and flour.

4. Mix in cheese and bacon rashers.

5. Put into a mediums sized quiche skillet.

6. Heat in an oven for 40 minutes.

7. Serve hot.

Tangy Salmon Quiche

This quiche is jam-packed with nutrients thanks to its filling of smoked salmon. You can prepare it quite easily and enjoy it with your friends or family.

Serving Size: 4

Duration: 50 minutes

List of Ingredients:

- 1 shallot, finely minced
- 3 eggs
- 1/4 cup lard
- 1 cup cheese, shredded
- 1 cup whole milk
- 1/2 a cup flour
- 1 tomato, chopped
- 1 cup smoked salmon, cubes
- 1/2 a cup parsley, finely minced

xxxxxxxxxxxxxxxxxxxxxxxxxxxxxxxxxxxxxxxxxxxxxxxxxxxxxxxx

Directions:

1. Put eggs and cheese in a blender and mix at low pulse.

2. Add in whole milk and continue on low pulse.

3. Season with sea salt and black pepper and set aside.

4. Put lard in a bowl and add in flour.

5. Put in the shallot. Add this to the first mixture and stir well.

6. Put mixture into and oiled quiche pan.

7. Place salmon cubes in the filling.

8. Add parsley followed by tomato.

9. Heat in an oven at 365°F for 40 minutes.

Spinach Swiss Quiche

This is a quiche recipe that belongs in a gourmet restaurant. However, it is very simple to prepare, and your guest will be bewildered when you will tell them that this is a home-cooked meal.

Serving Size: 4

Duration: 45 minutes

List of Ingredients:

- 1 pie pastry
- 4 bacon strips, finely chopped
- 1/4 cup shallots, finely chopped
- 1/4 cup sweet pepper, finely chopped
- 1 packet spinach, finely chopped
- 2 cups egg substitute
- 1/2 a cup cottage cheese
- 1/4 cup Swiss cheese, shredded
- 1/2 a tsp. dried oregano
- 1/4 tsp. dried parsley
- 1/4 tsp. paprika
- 1/4 tsp. black pepper
- 1/4 tsp. sea salt
- 6 tbsp. sour cream

xxxxxxxxxxxxxxxxxxxxxxxxxxxxxxxxxxxxxxxxxxxxxxxxxxxxxxxxx

Directions:

1. Place pastry on a work surface and then in a pie plate. Flute its edges.

2. Heat in an oven at 450°F for 10 minutes.

3. Cool on a wire rack. Reduce heat to 350°F.

4. In a small skillet, heat the bacon, shallot, and pepper.

5. When the veggies are tender; drain.

6. Stir in spinach. Put spinach mixture into pastry.

7. In a small pot, put in the egg substitute with cottage cheese.

8. Mix in Swiss cheese and seasonings.

9. Put this over the spinach mixture.

10. Heat in an oven for 40 minutes.

11. Place on a wire rack before cutting.

Canadian Bacon Shallot Quiche

The amazing blend of flavors in this quiche is mouthwatering indeed. Following this recipe, you will be able to cook this to perfection and amaze your guests with your culinary expertise.

Serving Size: 8

Duration: 50 minutes

List of Ingredients:

- 1 cup flour
- 1 tsp. sea salt
- 1/2 a cup lard
- 1/2 a cup cottage cheese
- 3 shallots, minced
- 4 ounces Canadian bacon, finely chopped
- 1/4 tsp. black pepper
- 3 eggs, lightly whisked
- 1 cup cheddar cheese, shredded

xxxxxxxxxxxxxxxxxxxxxxxxxxxxxxxxxxxxxxxxxxxxxxxxxxxxxxxxx

Directions:

1. First, preheat oven to 345°F.

2. In a small pot, stir flour and 1/4 tsp. sea salt; add lard.

3. Put in cottage cheese and shape into a disk.

4. On the work surface, roll dough into a circle, then put it in a pie plate and flute its edges.

5. In a wide skillet, heat remaining lard. Put in shallots; heat and stir until translucent.

6. Stir in bacon, black pepper, and salt.

7. Take off the heat and put in eggs followed by cheese.

8. Put everything into pastry shell.

9. Heat in an oven for 45 minutes.

10. Place on a wire rack before servings.

Tomato Infused Olive and Cheese Quiche Recipe

These amazing quiches will leave your guests and friends asking for more. The incredible aroma of tomatoes and Olives is appetizing indeed, and the taste of the dish does not disappoint.

Serving Size: 8

Duration: 40 minutes

List of Ingredients:

- 1 sheet pie pastry, thawed
- 1/4 cup flour
- 1/2 a tsp. sea salt
- 1/2 a tsp. black pepper
- 2 medium tomatoes, minced
- 2 tbsp. vegetable oil
- 2 eggs
- 1 cup cream
- 1 cup cheddar cheese, shredded
- 1 can olives, drained, pitted and finely diced
- 1 cup shallot, finely chopped
- 3 pieces Provolone cheese, sliced

Directions:

1. Place pastry into the pan.

2. Grease the shell with oil.

3. Heat in an oven at 450°F for 10 minutes.

4. Put in the flour, sea salt, and black pepper in a large pot.

5. Put in tomato and mix together.

6. In a wide skillet, heat tomatoes for 10 minutes.

7. In a separate pot, whisk together eggs with the cream; add cheddar cheese.

8. Spread olives and shallots in the crust; end with provolone cheese.

9. Add remaining tomatoes and the rest of provolone over the top.

10. Spread egg mixture on the finished pie at the end.

11. Heat in an oven at 375°F for 45 minutes.

12. Cool on a wire rack for 10 minutes.

Bacon and Cheese Quiche

This stunning meat-filled quiche combines the incredible taste of bacon with the smooth texture of the cheese. Each bite of this quiche is a heavenly gift to the taste buds.

Serving Size: 6

Duration: 45 minutes

List of Ingredients:

- 1 packet pie pastry
- 2 cups cooked bacon, finely chopped
- 2 cups cheddar cheese, shredded
- 2 tsp. dried shallot, finely minced
- 4 eggs
- 2 cups half-and-half
- 1/2 a tsp. sea salt
- 1/4 tsp. black pepper

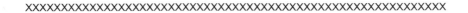

Directions:

1. Preheat oven to 390°F.

2. Place pastry sheets on a plate and trim edges.

3. Oil pastry shells. Fill with beans. Heat in an oven light golden.

4. Cool on wire racks.

5. Place bacon with the cheese and shallots in the shells.

6. In a wide pot, whisk eggs with cream. Season with sea salt and black pepper.

7. Add this to the shells.

8. Heat in an oven for 40 minutes.

9. Cool on a wire rack.

Cheesy Zucchini Quiche

This incredible quiche combines the tangy ate of zucchini with the smoothness of the cheese. Your masterful cooking will soon be the talk of the town with this incredible dish.

Serving Size: 6

Duration: 45 minutes

List of Ingredients:

- 1 Pie Pastry
- 3 tbsp. lard
- 4 cups zucchini, thinly chopped
- 1 shallot, thinly chopped
- 2 eggs
- 2 tsp. parsley, dried
- 1/2 a tsp. sea salt
- 1/2 a tsp. garlic, powdered
- 1/2 a tsp. basil, dried
- 1/2 a tsp. oregano, dried
- 1/4 tsp. black pepper
- 2 cups mozzarella cheese, shredded
- 2 tsp. mustard

xxxxxxxxxxxxxxxxxxxxxxxxxxxxxxxxxxxxxxxxxxxxxxxxxxxxxxxxx

Directions:

1. Preheat the kitchen oven to 390°F.

2. On a work surface, roll dough into a circle and place it in a pie plate.

3. Flute the edges and put in a fridge.

4. Heat lard in a wide skillet and put in zucchini slices with shallot. Heat and stir until cooked.

5. Whisk eggs with parsley, salt, garlic, basil, and oregano. Stir in the zucchini mix.

6. Put in mustard into pastry shell followed by filling.

7. Heat in an oven for 40 minutes.

8. Place on a wire rack before cutting.

Rainbow Quiche

This quiche is just like its name. It's a blend of incredible aromas and flavors that will be a pleasant surprise for almost everyone. The flavors create an explosion of taste in the mouth that is rivaled by only a few other dishes.

Serving Size: 8

Duration: 45 minutes

List of Ingredients:

- Single-crust pie pastry
- 2 tbsp. lard
- 1 small shallot, finely chopped
- 1 cup mushrooms, minced
- 1 cup broccoli, cut into small florets
- 1/2 a cup sweet pepper, finely chopped
- 1/2 a cup red pepper, finely chopped
- 1 cup baby spinach
- 3 eggs, lightly whisked
- 1 cup half-and-half
- 1 tsp. sea salt
- 1/2 a tsp. black pepper
- 1 cup Mexican cheese, shredded

xxxxxxxxxxxxxxxxxxxxxxxxxxxxxxxxxxxxxxxxxxxxxxxxxxxxxxx

Directions:

1. Preheat oven to 420°F.

2. Place pastry sheet work surface. Trim edges of the pastry and flute them.

3. In a wide skillet, heat lard over medium-high heat.

4. Heat shallots, mushrooms, and broccoli.

5. Add black peppers until mushrooms are golden.

6. Mix lightly beaten eggs with cream. Season with sea salt and black pepper.

7. Spread half a cup cheese over crust; add spinach and veggie mix.

8. Spread with remaining cheese. Put in egg mix.

9. Heat in an oven for half an hour.

10. Place on a wire rack to cool.

Bite-sized Sausage Quiches

These mini quiches pack a powerful punch. Filled with an incredible sausage filling, they taste heavenly, and their aroma is divine as well.

Serving Size: 4

Duration: 40 minutes

List of Ingredients:

- 1/2 a pound Italian sausage
- 2 tbsp. shallot, finely minced
- 2 tbsp. chives, finely minced
- 1 tube crescent rolls, thawed
- 4 eggs, lightly whisked
- 2 cups Swiss, cheese shredded
- 1 cup cottage cheese
- 1 cup Parmesan cheese, shredded
- 1 tsp. Paprika

xxxxxxxxxxxxxxxxxxxxxxxxxxxxxxxxxxxxxxxxxxxxxxxxxxxxxxxxx

Directions:

1. In a wide skillet, cook sausage and shallots 5 minutes. Drain when meat is tender.

2. Add the chives.

3. Lightly flour the word surface and place crescent dough on top.

4. Cut dough into four dozen pieces.

5. Place each into muffin cups.

6. Fill with 2 tsp. of cooked sausage mix.

7. In a wide pot, put in the farm eggs and both kinds of cheese.

8. Spread paprika on top.

9. Heat in an oven at 375°F for 25 minutes.

10. Cool on wire rack.

Mushroom Asparagus Quiche

This recipe has an incredible aroma, thanks to the liberal use of asparagus. The easy folding means that you will be able to delight your guest with this stunning meal at a moment's notice.

Serving Size: 8 servings

Duration: 50 minutes

List of Ingredients:

- 8 ounces crescent rolls, thawed
- 2 tsp. Dijon mustard
- 2 pounds asparagus, finely chopped
- 1 medium shallot, finely chopped
- 1/2 a cup organic mushrooms, minced
- 1/4 cup lard, cubed
- 2 eggs, lightly whisked
- 2 cups mozzarella cheese, shredded
- 1/4 cup organic parsley, finely minced
- 1/2 a tsp. sea salt
- 1/2 a tsp. black pepper
- 1/4 tsp. garlic, powdered
- 1/4 tsp. dried basil
- 1/4 tsp. oregano
- 1/4 tsp. rubbed sage

xxxxxxxxxxxxxxxxxxxxxxxxxxxxxxxxxxxxxxxxxxxxxxxxxxxxxxxxx

Directions:

1. Make 8 triangles with the thawed crescent dough, and place in a skillet.

2. Pinch both sides to create a crust. Put in mustard on top and let it rest.

3. Heat the asparagus in a wide skillet.

4. Put in shallot followed by mushrooms in lard.

5. Cook until the asparagus is half done.

6. In a wide pot, put in sage with oregano, and then put in dried basil with garlic.

7. Season with black pepper, sea salt, and parsley before adding cheese and eggs.

8. Stir together the remaining items; add asparagus mixture. Put this mixture into the crust.

9. Heat in an oven for 30 minutes at 375°F until the middle is also well done.

10. Let it rest for 10 minutes before slicing.

Spinach and Feta Quiche

This quiche combines Spinach and Feta with astounding results. It may be a bit complex to prepare the first time, but you will soon be able to create this dish with complete ease.

Serving Size: 4

Duration: 40 minutes

List of Ingredients:

- 1 puff pastry
- 4 eggs
- 1/2 a cup whole milk
- 1/3 cup feta
- 1/2 a cup spinach

Directions:

1. Preheat the kitchen oven to 380°F.

2. Line a quiche pan with pastry.

3. Heat spinach in a deep pan and let it rest for a while.

4. Add four eggs to a deep bowl and whisk

5. Add milk to eggs and stir.

6. Add spinach to the quiche pan.

7. Spread the feta on the pastry crust.

8. Heat in an oven for 30 minutes.

9. Cool on a wire rack.

Vegan Bacon Quiche

Who says that vegans cannot enjoy bacon? This visually stunning quiche with its vegan-inspired filling is a treat for all vegans who want to enjoy quiche but are unable to do so due to the lack of options in fillings.

Serving Size: 4

Duration: 40 minutes

List of Ingredients:

- 1 Pie Dough, uncooked
- 2 tbsp. oil
- 1 cup shallot, finely minced
- 4 cloves garlic, finely minced
- 4 ounces vegan bacon, finely minced
- 1 tsp. sea salt
- 1/4 tsp. pepper flakes
- 2 cups broccoli, broken into florets
- 1 pound tofu
- 2 tbsp. lime juice
- 1 tbsp. Tahini
- 1 tbsp. rice vinegar
- 8 ounces Vegan Cheese, shredded

XXXXXXXXXXXXXXXXXXXXXXXXXXXXXXXXXXXXXXXXXXXXXXXXXXXXX

Directions:

1. Roll out the pie dough and place it in the quiche pan.

2. Preheat the oven to 355°F.

3. Add oil to a skillet and put in shallots. Heat until light brown.

4. Add, garlic and vegan bacon. Continue to stir and cook.

5. Season with sea salt and pepper flakes

6. Take off the stove and let it rest.

7. Steam broccoli florets for 5 minutes.

8. Add them to the shallots and toss.

9. Toss with the shallot-vegan bacon mixture and let it rest.

10. Blend tofu with lemon juice at low pulse.

11. Add Tahini and rice vinegar.

12. Add broccoli and shallots to the blended mixture and stir.

13. Spread vegan cheese on the dough.

14. Put in the filling.

15. Heat in an oven for 50 minutes.

Mountain Bread Quiche

This quiche is a twist on the traditional mountain bread pie. Its filling of turkey and mushroom combined with its seasoning create an incredible taste and a mouthwatering aroma.

Serving Size: 1

Duration: 30 minutes

List of Ingredients:

- 1 mountain bread
- 1/4 cup zucchini, finely diced
- 1/4 cup sweet potato
- 1 mushroom, finely diced
- 1 slice turkey, finely chopped
- 1 egg, lightly whisked
- 1 tbsp. whole milk
- 1 tbsp. cheese, shredded

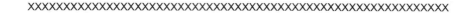

xxxxxxxxxxxxxxxxxxxxxxxxxxxxxxxxxxxxxxxxxxxxxxxxxxxxxxxxxxx

Directions:

1. Preheat oven to 360°F.

2. Oil a quiche pan and line it mountain bread.

3. In a deep pot, combine zucchini with sweet potato.

4. Mix in mushroom and turkey.

5. Crack in the egg and add milk and cheese.

6. Put the mixture into the quiche pan.

7. Heat in an oven for 30 minutes.

8. Cool on a wire rack and serve warm.

Broccoli Quiche

This vegan quiche is a godsend for those who follow the vegan diet. Its broccoli filling is infused with cheese to deliver an amazing combination of flavors.

Serving Size: 4

Duration: 40 minutes

List of Ingredients:

- 1 pie crust, uncooked
- 1 tbsp. vegetable oil
- 1 shallot, finely chopped
- 2 cups broccoli, cut into florets
- 6 eggs
- 1 cup cheddar cheese, finely grated
- 1 cup half and half
- 1/2 a tsp. sea salt
- 1/4 tsp. pepper

xxxxxxxxxxxxxxxxxxxxxxxxxxxxxxxxxxxxxxxxxxxxxxxxxxxxxxxx

Directions:

1. Preheat the kitchen oven to 380°F.

2. Heat crust in the oven for about 10 minutes.

3. Heat oil in a skillet and add shallots.

4. Add broccoli florets and cheese to the quiche crust. Let it rest.

5. In deep pot, beat 3 eggs lightly and add yolks. Add in half and half.

6. Season with salt and pepper.

7. Put filling in the crust.

8. Heat in an oven for 40 minutes.

9. Cool on a wire rack before serving.

Gourmet Quiche

This is a complex quiche dish. However, once you master this dish, you will be able to cook this stunning Michelin-level dish right in your own kitchen.

Serving Size: 3

Duration: 50 minutes

List of Ingredients:

- 5 eggs
- 1/2 a tsp. pepper
- 1/4 tsp. sea salt
- 1/4 tsp. garlic powder
- 1 cup soy milk
- 6 ounces Vegan Gourmet Cheddar, shredded
- 2 cups spinach, chopped

xxxxxxxxxxxxxxxxxxxxxxxxxxxxxxxxxxxxxxxxxxxxxxxxxxxxxxxx

Directions:

1. Preheat the oven to 360°F.

1. In a deep pot, whisk the eggs with pepper, sea salt, and garlic powder.

2. Add soy milk and whisk until smooth. Then let it rest.

3. Spread half of the cheese into a quiche pan.

4. Add the remaining to egg bowl.

5. Put in spinach and stir.

6. Add filling to the dough.

7. Heat in an oven for 35 minutes.

8. Cool on a wire rack.

Minced Beef Quiche

This quiche will be highly appreciated by all the fans of beef. Its amazing filling of minced beef is infused with an incredible blend of spices to create a heavenly taste.

Serving Size: 4

Duration: 50 minutes

List of Ingredients:

- 1 pound beef, minced
- 1 shallot, finely chopped
- 1 tbsp. oil
- 1/2 a tsp. sea salt
- 1/2 a tsp. dried oregano
- 1/2 a tsp. garlic powder
- 1/4 tsp. pepper
- 3 eggs
- 1/2 a cup whole milk
- 1/2 a cup mayo
- 1 cup cheddar cheese, shredded
- 1 cup Swiss cheese, shredded
- 1 sheet puff pastry

xxxxxxxxxxxxxxxxxxxxxxxxxxxxxxxxxxxxxxxxxxxxxxxxxxxxxxxxx

Directions:

1. Heat vegetable oil in a flat skillet.

2. Add beef and shallots and heat until golden brown. Take off heat and set aside.

3. In a deep pot, beat the eggs.

4. Add whole milk and mayo to the mix and stir well.

5. Add meat and put in cheddar cheese with Swiss cheese.

6. Season with sea salt and oregano.

7. Sprinkle garlic powder and pepper.

8. Place puff pastry in an oiled quiche pan. Put in dollops of the mixture.

9. Heat in an oven at 390°F for 45 minutes.

10. Rest on a wire rack before serving.

Asparagus Turmeric Quiche

This quiche delivers a stunning combination of asparagus and turmeric in its filling. Your guests will be singing your praises with each bite of this scrumptious dish.

Serving Size: 8

Duration: 50 minutes

List of Ingredients:

- 1/2 a pound asparagus
- Vegetable oil
- 1/2 a tsp. sea salt
- 1/2 a tsp. black pepper
- 8 ounces Vegan Gourmet Cheddar, shredded
- 25 ounces tofu
- 1/2 a cup soy milk
- 1/4 cup nutritional yeast
- 3 tbsp. cashews, finely chopped
- 3 tbsp. cornstarch
- 1/2 a tsp. garlic powder
- 1/2 a tsp. shallot powder
- 1/4 tsp. turmeric

xxxxxxxxxxxxxxxxxxxxxxxxxxxxxxxxxxxxxxxxxxxxxxxxxxxx

Directions:

1. Grill the asparagus.

2. Lightly season with sea salt and black pepper

3. Take off from the grill, chop and Let it rest.

4. Preheat the oven to 360°F.

5. Spread cheese in the quiche pan.

6. Add asparagus on the cheese.

7. In a blender mix, tofu with soy milk at low pulse.

8. Add in yeast and turmeric.

9. Mix in cornstarch and shallot powder.

10. Add garlic powder and the rest of cheese.

11. Mix in ground cashews.

12. Put the filling into the quiche pan.

13. Heat in an oven 40 minutes.

14. Cool on a wire rack.

Spinach and Ricotta Quiche

The Spinach and Ricotta Quiche is considered to be a complex dish to cook, given the variety of the ingredients used. However, this simple recipe will allow you to cook this Spanish dish to perfection.

Serving Size: 4

Duration: 40 minutes

List of Ingredients:

- 1 shallot, finely chopped
- 3 garlic cloves, finely chopped
- 1 tbsp. vegetable oil
- 4 eggs
- 1 cup spinach, chopped
- 1 cup ricotta
- 1/2 a cup cream
- 1/2 a cup cheddar cheese, shredded
- 1/2 a cup whole milk
- 1 tbsp. sea salt.
- 1 tbsp. black pepper
- 2 puff pastries

xxxxxxxxxxxxxxxxxxxxxxxxxxxxxxxxxxxxxxxxxxxxxxxxxxxxxx

Directions:

1. Preheat oven to 360°F.

2. Heat the oil in a flat pan.

3. Put in the shallot and garlic. Cook until brown.

4. Beat the eggs in a deep pot. Put in the spinach and ricotta.

5. Stir in cheese and cream.

6. Add milk and season with sea salt and black pepper.

7. Add shallot and garlic mix. Stir well.

8. Roll out pastry in an oiled quiche pan.

9. Add the filling.

10. Heat in an oven for 35 minutes.

11. Cool on wire rack before serving.

Paleo Quiche

This incredible quiche is a delight for all those who follow the Paleo diet. Its simple filling of eggs makes it a highly nutritious meal that can be served to children and health-conscious adults alike.

Serving Size: 4

Duration: 40 minutes

List of Ingredients:

- 1/2 a cup soy margarine
- 1 pie dough, uncooked
- 9 eggs
- 1/2 a cup plain flour
- 3 and a half cups almond milk
- 1/4 cup nutritional yeast
- 2 tsp. sea salt

xxxxxxxxxxxxxxxxxxxxxxxxxxxxxxxxxxxxxxxxxxxxxxxxxxxxxxx

Directions:

1. Preheat the kitchen oven to 380°F.

2. Oil a quiche pan with soy margarine.

3. Roll out the pie dough on a work surface. Place it in the quiche pan.

4. Beat 1 egg and add flour. Whisk until smooth.

5. Put in the remaining eggs and beat until frothy.

6. Put in almond milk and slowly add yeast.

7. Put in sea salt and continue to stir

8. Put the mixture into crust.

9. Heat in an oven for 15 minutes.

10. Turn down the heat to 320°F.

11. Heat for 40 minutes more.

12. Cool on a wire rack before serving.

Author's Afterthoughts

I can't appreciate you enough for spending your precious time reading my book. If there is anything that gladdens an author's heart, it is that his or her work be read. And I am extremely joyous that my labor and the hours put into making this publication a reality didn't go to waste.

Another thing that gladdens an author's heart is feedback because every comment from the good people who read one's book matters a great deal in helping you become better at what you do.

This is why I wouldn't shy away from reading your thoughts and comments about what you have read in this publication.

Do you think it is good enough? Do you think it could be better?

Please keep the feedback coming in, I won't hesitate to read any of them!!!

Thanks!

Layla Tacy

Biography

Climbing up the ladder from a young girl who loved to experiment with food items in her mother's cottage kitchen at the tender age of 7, to changing cooking from what it was to what it should be; Layla has more than made a name for herself, but she has created a dynasty for herself in the cooking world.

With more than twenty-five years in the culinary world, Layla has grown to be an authority with her influence spreading all over different high-class hotels and restaurants in and around Kansas City, such as Hilton President Kansas City, The Fountaine hotel, and Embassy Suites.

After working as a chef in different establishments, Layla moved on to become a chef-trainer to several up-and-coming chefs. Currently, she has graduated more than 200 trainees at her Chef School and presently has about 150 graduates in her school.